Let Me Love You One Day at a Time

Let Me Love You
One Day at a Time

Hallmark Editions

Let me love you one day at a time ...

... and please love me that very same way.

We may never learn

all there is to know about love...

... but every day together
    will teach us
        a little more about ourselves
  and the special kind of happiness
    we can bring to each other.

One of the best things you've helped me learn
is that love starts with being honest ...
speaking straight from how we really feel.

I like how we've opened the doors
and windows of our lives
and invited each other to come in,
look around and get acquainted ...

... and the more I'm with you,

the more at home I feel.

Let me love you one day at a time.
Why talk about "always"
and say things we're not sure we mean
when we can talk about today
and mean exactly
what we say?

Let's think of each sunrise as a fresh start,
a brand-new beginning ...

... and try to fill every day
with as much love
as it can hold.

I know you're not always going to be
exactly the same person
Sunday through Saturday,
January through December ...
and neither am I.

We both need laughing times

and crying times ...

... and times for every other mood in between.

The important thing
is that you can be
the kind of you
that feels most natural ...
and that I can be
my favorite kind of me.

That's what makes us

so comfortable together ...

*... it's also what keeps us
    from taking each other
    too much for granted.*

Let me love you one day at a time.
Let's not wonder how long love will last
but how beautiful
we can make it grow.

Let's give our best to each other,

but let's never expect miracles of our love.

There's no need to ...

... the reality of you and me
is better
than all the impossible dreams
and fantasies
I've ever imagined.

Being with you
   is feeling proud, blessed, grateful
   for each hour we share.

Let me love you,

not according to any how-to book

or by someone else's set of rules ...

*... but simply for who you are
and how you are with me.*

And please love me,
  not for what I ought to be
or for what I might be molded into,
  but for what I am, here and now.

Don't expect me to be

someone all good and all giving,

someone who could never disappoint you ...

... someone too right to be real

and too perfect to be me.

I'm just as human as anyone I know ...

and very thankful that you are, too.

Let's try to remember
*   that love means keeping in touch*
with each other's thoughts
and feelings ...

... listening, not just to words,

but to the emotions behind them ...

... seeing, not just the smiles and frowns,
but the hurts and pleasures
that cause them.

Let me love you one day at a time, starting today.
Let's have the courage to try to change
whatever needs changing about us
and the wisdom to know
what should never be changed.

Let's not worry about what went wrong yesterday.
Let's help each other make today
as right as it can be ...

... believing in ourselves

and in our ability to handle

whatever tomorrow may bring ...

... and trusting that this love we share
will continue to grow stronger
as the future years unfold ...
one beautiful day at a time.

Let Me Love You One Day at a Time
was written by Edward Cunningham.
The typeface is Plantin italic designed
for monotype by F. H. Pierpont.
Book design and title page calligraphy
by Rick Cusick. The designer
gratefully acknowledges Dale Durfee
for her assistance.

PHOTOGRAPHS: Dale Durfee, frontispiece, pages
5, 8, 17, 25, 28, 33, 37, 44; Keith Carey, title page,
pages 12, 41, 45; Harv Gariety, page 20.